Gallery Books
Editor Peter Fallon

FOR ALL WE KNOW

Ciaran Carson

FOR ALL
WE KNOW

Gallery Books

For All We Know
is first published
simultaneously in paperback
and in a clothbound edition
on 13 March 2008.

The Gallery Press
Loughcrew
Oldcastle
County Meath
Ireland

www.gallerypress.com

ISBN 978 1 85235 439 8 *paperback*
    978 1 85235 440 4 *clothbound*

A CIP catalogue record for this book
is available from the British Library.

Contents

La nuit s'approche et mon village
S'endort là-bas silencieux
La cloche sonne, et son langage
Annonce le fin des adieux

Quand vient le soir après l'orage
Fuyons, prenons le droit sentier
Adieu les rêves de jeune âge
Anges, gardez notre foyer
                                        — Old song

Night approaches and my village/ Slumbers over there in silence/ The bell rings, and its language/ Announces the end of farewells
    When evening comes after storm/ Let us flee, let us take the right path/ Farewell the dreams of youthful days/Angels, watch over our hearth

Fugue must perform its frequently stealthy work with continuously shifting melodic fragments that remain, in the 'tune' sense, perpetually unfinished.
— Glenn Gould
'So You Want to Write a Fugue'

for Deirdre
comme toujours

PART ONE

Second Time Round

Ce n'est pas comme le pain de Paris. There's no stretch in it,
you said. It was our anniversary, whether first or last.

It's the matter of the texture. Elasticity.
The crust should crackle when you break the *baton*. Then you pull

the crumb apart to make skeins full of holes. I was grappling
with your language over the wreck of the dining table.

The maitre d' was looking at us in a funny way
as if he caught the drift I sought between the lines you spoke.

For one word never came across as just itself, but you
would put it over as insinuating something else.

Then slowly, slowly we would draw in on one another
until everything was implicated like wool spooled

from my yawning hands as you wound the yarn into a ball.
For how many seasons have we circled round each other

like this? Was it because you came from there and I from here?
That said, before we were a gleam in someone else's eye?

Behind the screen of reasons, how much further back we go.
La nuit s'approche, you said, and then I saw the parish church

below the Alps of those three words, and snow falling, a bell
tolling as their farewells dimmed into the gathering dusk.

Our two candles were guttering by now. We climbed the stair
and found ourselves spreadeagled on the patchwork double quilt

following the dips and gradients of the staggered repeats
four widow aunts had stitched into it fifty years before

the last war, one of them your ancestor. So they told you
as you told me that day in Paris we two first ventured

under it, into the future we would make together
there and then, the bread you bought that morning not yet broke

Hotel del Mar

Sound of waves without. You were abroad and ignorant in
the tongue you heard whispering from a dinner table more

than one remove away from you, two pairs of lips closing
in on one another in the flickering candlelight —

murmuring of sweet nothings, you surmised, since it was Greek
to you. Waves on the beach. Did we two, you wondered, ever

come across like that? Some lonely traveller to overhear
words not understood, a shadow on the periphery?

Whatever window opened then, moonlight shivered on you,
the gold crushed velvet curtains stirred in the breeze off the sea.

The couple spoke more boldly now, as if you were not there.
So you told it that I might fathom the deep of its sound,

we two seas foundering into one another over
the neck of a peninsula, making it an island.

On the Contrary

It's because we were brought up to lead double lives, you said.
You were lying next to me, both of us verging on sleep.

We always had to withhold ourselves from the other side,
guarding our tongues lest we answer to their outspoken laws.

And so we lost ourselves in the dark forest of language
believing in nothing which might not be governed by touch

or taste, the apple bursting indescribably with juice
against the roof of the mouth, or the clean cold smell of skin.

As our promise was never to be betrayed by our words
so we became our own shadowy police watching us,

as loaded the long goods train clanks slowly towards Dublin,
we hear the shriek in the night from across the trip-wired fields,

as the searchlight trawls across the bedroom window you turn
towards me speechlessly and we look into each other's eyes.

Treaty

It's like putting yourself in someone else's shoes, you said,
or checking into a hotel under another name

except back home you need them to believe in the fiction.
For this is not a strange country where you are free to be

whosoever you like, to bask in the equable sun
in happy ignorance of the language. There you are not.

Remember those radiating pathways of Versailles where
you confessed yourself happy to be known to none but me?

Whereas here the insignia are all too familiar
and country roads are walked in circumspection to music

in order to encompass the other's territory —
this story we've been over so many times, inventing

that which we might have been had we been born as another,
as truly we tell them a name that sounds like one of theirs.

Redoubt

If only because in another country you are free
to renegotiate yourself or what you thought you were,

I found myself this night approached by a man in a suit.
When he asked me what I was drinking I didn't demur.

French was a lingua franca. He showed me a worn photo,
wife and children smiling at us from some Polish city.

We'd already exchanged names, whatever they were. So what
did I do? I told him I was a writer, not well known.

Me? I'm a salesman, he said, I travel in fountain pens.
He represented all the big companies like Mont Blanc.

It was the coming back-to-the-future thing in the East,
though back where I come from, he said, they'd never gone away.

But what they desired now was 'Western exclusivity'.
And what sort of thing do you write, would you like to try mine?

Even before he proffered it I knew it was a fake.
He'd filled it with fancy ink. *De l'encre violette.*

So I wrote I was a writer of fiction and poems,
and if you're about to ask me what they're about, I said,

that's for the reader to say, whose guess is as good as mine.
He smiled. And how did it all end up? I said, picturing

the scene, bottles with strange labels glinting in the background,
the bartender pretending to polish a glass, and you

looking the Mont Blanc man in the eye. I imagined snow
outside, the footsteps that brought you there already erased

as were his that crossed yours at the threshold if not before,
as we two were strangers to each other when we first met.

I stared at my face for an age in the en suite mirror.
Then I must have crawled into bed before my mind went blank.

The Assignation

I think I must have told him my name was Juliette,
with four syllables, you said, to go with *violette*.

I envisaged the violet air that presages snow,
the dark campaniles of a city beginning to blur

a malfunctioning violet neon pharmacy sign
jittering away all night through the dimity curtains.

Near dawn you opened them to a deep fall and discovered
a line of solitary footprints leading to a porch:

a smell of candle-wax and frankincense; the dim murmur
of a liturgy you knew but whose language you did not.

The statues were shrouded in Lenten violet, save one,
a Virgin in a cope of voile so white as to be blue.

As was the custom there, your host informed you afterwards —
the church was dedicated to Our Lady of the Snows.

Revolution

Then I would try to separate the grain from the chaff of
helicopter noise as it hovered above on my house.

This was back in the late Sixties, I didn't know you then.
Later I'd picture you in an apartment in Paris.

You'd be watching riot police and students on TV,
banners and barbed wire unfurling across the boulevards

and the air thick with stones. The helicopters came later
within earshot grinding the sound-bites into vocables.

I felt I had a malfunctioning cochlear implant,
that someone I didn't know was watching me from on high.

The picture would break up into unreadable pixels.
I'd imagine putting my lips to the door of your ear

as I held the conch you brought back from Ithaca to mine,
listening to shells becoming shingle, and shingle sand.

Through

Irrevocable? Never irrevocable, you said,
picking me up wrong through the din of the coffee machine.

We were in the Ulster Milk Bar I think they blew up back
in the Seventies. We must have been barely acquainted.

Noise is what surrounds us, I'd said earlier, gesturing
to the wider world of disinformation, the dizzy

spells that come when someone you know might have been in a
  bomb
as the toll has not yet been reckoned except by hearsay.

I'd have my ear glued to the radio, waiting for what
passed for the truth to come out, men picking through the rubble

Some of the victims would appear in wedding photographs
blinded by a light forever gone. Graveside by graveside

I shake hands with men I have not shaken hands with for years,
trying to make out their faces through what they have become.

Pas de Deux

It all began in Take Two, what with us looking at clothes.
You'd brushed against me as I stepped aside from the mirror

to let you size yourself up against a blue pencil skirt,
pinching its waistband to your waist with your arms akimbo.

I caught you taking me in from the corner of your eye
as I fingered the nap on a Donegal tweed jacket.

Nice jacket, you said. Yes? I said. Yes, you said, I love that
Harris tweed, the heathery feel of the handwoven wool.

You're not from around here, I said. No, from elsewhere, you said.
As from another language, I might have said, but did not.

Though your English was perfect I couldn't place the accent
and you'd put things in such a way no native would have done.

N'a pas fait qui commence, you came to say later, only
begun is not done. And so it was we got acquainted,

as with the glow of our cigarettes we'd scrawl neon signs
to each other on the dark, the words fading instantly

as written, comprehended by the eye in retrospect
as over us a helicopter drowned conversation.

That was the kind of spin that passed for dialogue back then,
one side revolving the other's words for other meanings,

or sidestepping the issue, demanding actions instead.
It took us some time to establish our identity,

for you'd learned where you came from to choose your words
  carefully.
And often you'd seal my lips with a kiss as silently

under a blanket we'd struggle into one another
to end up sleeping like two naked spoons or back to back,

the second-hand pencil skirt on your side of the wardrobe,
the second-hand tweed jacket brushing against it on mine.

Second Hand

Nice watch, I said. Yes, you said, Omega. White gold bezel
with black guilloche enamel inlay. Porcelain dial.

Arabic numerals, alpha hands. Seventeen jewel
movement. Pre-War, all original — look, it's even got

the original black silk ribbon band. Butterfly clasp.
You turned your wrist to show me as you spoke. How long ago

was that? I knew you a matter of minutes back then; now
it's years. As it turned out your uncle collected watches.

This one had been your aunt's. He'd take off the back of a watch
to show how it worked, levers, gears, bearings, wheels, screws and
   springs

registering elapsed time with a dispassionate tick.
You held it to my ear. I listened to the seconds pass

as now I listen to the wind on this cold starry night,
and I wonder if your Omega watch is working still.

Le Mot Juste

Still the interminable wrestle with words and meanings?
you said. I'd an idea you were quoting from something.

But from what? Rather than answer, I put my pen aside
and poured the miniature jug of milk into my coffee.

You watched over it quizzically as it became *au lait.*
Wouldn't you rather talk about your day? I said at length.

I practised a little Well-Tempered Clavier, you said,
and I envisioned your nimble fingers on the keyboard.

The C-minor prelude and the B-minor fugue, you said,
the two ends of the book as it were. I've often wondered

how many quills Bach went through over those twenty-two
    years.
Do you know that Bach had twenty children? I do, I said.

You reached suddenly across the table to put your mouth
to mine, murmuring what I took for a fugue on my lips.

Proposal

You were one of the first to go for an Apple, when they
first came out, you said, it must have been the year whenever,

1984? Stuck, you'd click on the Option button
whereupon up popped a menu of possible answers

through which you dropped down until it took your mind to the
    end
you so desired, the Tree of Knowledge looming within reach.

All too soon you were plucking data from the air, making
documents, files and spreadsheets, putting your life in order.

We'd climb into bed to the noise of a helicopter
to bury our selves under the clothes to muffle the beat

with the beat of our synchronized hearts. When all was done but
not said, you'd speak temptingly of the serendipity

of the Apple, how it seemed to put words into your mouth
to say what you wanted to say but could not until then.

The Shadow

You know how you know when someone's telling lies? you said.
    They
get their story right every time, down to the last word.

Whereas when they tell the truth it's never the same twice. They
reformulate. The day in question and whatever passed

between them and the other can be seen so many ways,
the way they sometimes ask themselves if it happened at all.

All this was *à propos* of your first time in East Berlin.
The Wall was not long down. It was Easter 1990,

you found yourself in a place in Herman-Hesse-Strasse.
You were alone in the dining room one evening, reading

The Glass Bead Game over *Bierwurst*, sauerkraut and a draught be‹
when the middle-aged waiter approached you from the shadows

Bitte, he said; may I? You gestured towards an empty chair.
You wouldn't remember how the talk took the turn it did,

but however it happened his life began to come out.
He'd set up two schnapps by then. He'd been in the Stasi once.

The lie is memorized, the truth is remembered, he said.
I learned that early on in their school before I became

interrogator. That was after I learned to listen
in. They played many tapes of many stories, some true, some

false. I was asked to identify which was which, and where
the conversations might have taken place, whatever time.

And the ones who sobbed over and over, I am telling
the truth, never changed their story, he said. End of story.

You've told me this story more than once, more than once telling
me something I never heard before until then, telling

it so well I could almost believe I was there myself,
for all that I was at the time so many miles away.

The Fetch

To see one's own doppelganger is an omen of death.
The doppelganger casts no reflection in a mirror.

Shelley saw himself swimming towards himself before he
    drowned.
Lincoln met his fetch at the stage door before he was shot.

It puts me in mind of prisoners interrogated,
of one telling his story so well he could see himself

performing in it, speaking the very words he spoke now,
seeing the face of the accomplice he had invented.

When all is said and done there is nothing more to be said.
No need for handcuffs, or any other restraint. They take

a swab of his sweat from the vinyl chair in which he sat.
Should he ever escape his prison the dogs shall be loosed.

Your death stands always in the background, but don't be afraid.
For he will only come to fetch you when your time has come.

Second Take

Most of the witnesses we knew then are dead if not gone,
sequestered in havens to become shadows of themselves.

Take Carrick, whose name was a byword for integrity,
bundled into an unmarked car to vanish without trace:

whatever he'd borne witness to must have been worth knowing,
so much so they say he arranged his own disappearance.

Take McCloud, a man notoriously hard of hearing,
whose earpiece was tuned to every whisper in the city:

he fell foul of a so-called cancer of the inner ear,
a steady creep of secrets invading the labyrinth.

Take the others who were given a new identity,
not that we could say for sure who they were in the first place.

Take me, you said, the first time ever you set eyes on me:
for all that I told you then, you took me for what I was.

Corrigendum

I put what you call a bug in all of the light switches,
said the Stasi man, to entrap the couple by their words.

Their names had been put forward as what you call dissenters,
so I listened to all they had to say to each other.

There were long periods of silence but for the TV
and I won't say what they did when all was dark and silent,

and for all that they quarrelled they never raised their voices,
which by itself might be construed as evidence of guilt.

So many schnapps later the Stasi man was on the verge
of oblivion. His last words were, Do you believe me?

I nodded as if I did. I reached a loose-leaf notebook
from my handbag and asked if he would write his name. He did.

When I came to the next day and tried to make sense of it
all the pages were blank and I never saw him again.

Fall

So what do you do? I said. We'd just exchanged names. I do
what you might call cultural *journalisme*, you replied.

It was windy that day and when it rained the sun came out.
Raindrops, leaf-shadow dappled and spattered the blue cobbles.

Two pigeons clucked. The butcher's lay at the end of the block.
We were standing some seven doors down. You're not covering

the Troubles? I said. I watched your lips frame a silent No
as the bomb went off at the end of the block and drowned all

conversation. All the more difficult to find the words
for what things have been disrupted by aftershock and shock,

a fall of glass still toppling from the astonished windows,
difficult to ponder how we met, if it was for this.

From this we averted our eyes as we skirted the crowd,
the sirens dwindling into silence as we walked away.

L'Air du Temps

Nice perfume, I said. Thank you, you said. It was our first date.
I've always wondered about perfumes, I said, what is it?

L'Air du Temps by Nina Ricci, you said, she made it up
just after the War. Spirit of the Times, it was supposed

to evoke the era, the girls in Pompadour hairstyles
blowing kisses everywhere, garlanding the tank turrets.

Lalique designed the flacon later, 1951,
the frosted glass stopper a pair of intertwining doves.

As for the scent, it opens with luminous bergamot
and rosewood, developing a bouquet of gardenia,

violet, jasmine and ylang ylang. Wraiths of green moss
and sandalwood give L'Air du Temps its gentle persistence.

The base is powdery orris, cool woods, musk and resins,
permeated with a faint radiant heat of amber.

They say it goes well with pastels and purples, the latter
in every shade from palest lavender to heliotrope.

Fabrics should be near transparent, or crisp and clean, you said.
You were wearing a 1950s blouse of pastel blue.

So what shade would you call that? I said, looking at your blouse
You looked down at yourself. It's a very, very pale French

blue, you said. It puts me in mind of winters in Paris.
It is frosty, and if you stand in Montmartre you can

see for miles. I'm looking at the patchwork quilt of Paris:
parks, avenues, cemeteries, temples, impasses, arcades.

I can see the house where I was raised, and my mother's house.
I am in her boudoir looking at her in the mirror

as she, pouting, not looking, puts on L'Air du Temps, a spurt
of perfume on each wrist before she puts her wristwatch on.

Never Never

You were telling me a story of your great-grandmother's
over a bottle of Burgundy by a bubbling fire.

Deep in the Forest of Language there dwelt a manikin
not called Rumpelstiltskin. His name was not that important.

One day a riderless mare came trotting up to his door.
The manikin brought her to stable and fed her some hay.

He was surprised when the mare upped and spoke in the
    King's French.
I am not a mare, she said, but the King's daughter bewitched.

And because you have fed and stabled me I shall become
princess again. And she changed as she spoke before his eyes.

In return you have three wishes. I only want one wish,
said the manikin. I'm a manikin. Make me a man.

The by now fully-formed beautiful woman blinked at him
and in the blank and pupil of her eye he became man.

You took a long sip of wine. And what happened then? I said.
The princess summoned a horse from nowhere and galloped
    home.

The man walked to a great city. He became a joiner.
He grew skilled at his trade and his heart was in all he made.

He grew justly famous for his miniature chests of drawers,
each crafted from a plank of his oak house in the forest.

But still he pined for the day that he'd set the princess free.
He never looked at a woman until the day he died,

his last wish to be buried in the Forest of Language,
his body to be laid in a box of his own device.

To this day if you happen to pass that shadowy glade
you may see a ghostly rider riding a ghostly mare.

You lit a cigarette. And as for the princess? I said.
She married an English prince, you said, and got beheaded.

Birthright

Again you are trapped in the smouldering streets. Knots of men
armed with axes, files and chisels guard the intersections.

For all that you avert your gaze you know they know your kind.
The city wards have long been sealed and there is no escape.

For all that you assumed a sevenfold identity
the mark of your people's people blazes on your forehead.

You will be questioned by the black stream of the shibboleth,
your story picked like a cheap lock until it comes unstuck.

Whatever happens to you next is nothing personal.
What is written has been written, these the words on the page.

You will be taken down to the ironmonger's cellar
to be stood blindfolded before the splintered deal table

where seven inquisitors prepare a sentence to be
rasped out in the light of your inextinguishable name.

Collaboration

I am being paraded through the streets with my head shaved,
with no memory of what I have done to deserve this.

I run a gauntlet of women who call me slut and whore,
staggering under their fusillade of accusation:

What stories did I tell, what lies? What names did I reveal?
What men did I sleep with? What did I do? For what reward?

Or in a catacomb deep under Paris they press gloves
of barbed wire onto my bare hands, and when the wounds have
      healed

they point to the brambles left on my palms, saying, Surely
these lines of head and heart and mind are those of a traitor.

When you wake I hold you tight, saying, It's only a dream,
the language of dream has nothing to do with that of life.

And as eventually you sink back into the deep well
of sleep, I wonder if by my words I have betrayed you.

From Your Notebook

Dresden evening, then dusk. Linnets exploding over
the ruins of the *Frauenkirche*. They are building it

back stone by stone, the stones blackened as if in a coal fire,
every one of them numbered. This is all done according

to the still extant blueprints. The *Frauenkirche* will rise
from the ashes and be restored to its former glory.

Now I remember church music murmured in the background,
the muted hum of an organ playing under stained glass.

My glass of red wine flickers in the candlelight. It's dark
by now, the other tables empty. A waiter stands by.

I will finish this postcard in the hotel. Now I am
in my room writing this by the light of a Dresden lamp

whose base I take to be a Dresden figurine of Hope,
holding her bright orb aloft under a parchment lampshade.

Prelude and Fugue

They took me to a *Bierkeller* and fed me a ham hock.
I washed it down with cold Pilsener. Boisterous music

on the go, a man with a trombone in a pork-pie hat.
My host is sketching me a Bach prelude on a napkin.

He wrote this while in Dresden. Would you like somewhere quiet?
So we go upstairs to the ground floor where we find a snug.

The fugue that follows has some interesting dissonances.
I found myself gazing at the optics in the mirror.

Something else was going on. There was a jukebox in back.
You know this song? I nodded that I did in time to it.

He nodded back. There is something of the carol in it.
Then he told me how the candle-flares were like Christmas trees,

and so to the zoo where a keeper was running amok
among the burning monkeys and the teetering giraffes.

The Story of the Chevalier

I was walking away from the war across a white plain.
No one on the road behind me, nor on the road before.

A mare galloped out of nowhere with her reins trailing blood.
She halted beside me and nodded for me to get on.

We travelled towards the dark forest and reached it by nightfall.
Snow was in the air, but not here where no stars could be seen.

Her hooves picked out a meticulous path under the trees.
By happenstance she led me to the woodcutter's cottage.

I was just about to open the door when it opened.
I walked into the dark until my eyes got used to it.

When I looked back into the dark outside the mare had gone.
I turned into the other dark and saw you standing there.

Your dark hair was as it is now, tumbled to your shoulder,
and bore two scarlet ribbons I had never seen before.

To

Remember the fountain pen rep you met in wherever?
I said. Dresden, you said. I thought it was Berlin, I said.

I'd just come from there, you said. The Wall was not that long
    down.
For all that I dressed the part, a grey Eastern suit with skirt —

I wore a hat — I felt people were looking through me to
the *Ausländer* I was. But I safely boarded the train.

I'd exchanged no words with anyone bar the ticket clerk.
The dining-car said *Spiesewagen* in Black Letter script.

I looked it up and found that *Spiese* meant fare, as in food.
The carriages were all compartments and side corridors,

and the passengers did a lot of walking up and down,
so much so I thought I might draw attention to myself.

So I put the dictionary away and ventured to
the *Spiesewagen*, door after sliding door. That was when

I first saw him. He was faring on dark bread and blond beer.
A book with a German title lay face down before him.

I sat down two tables away somewhat unsteadily.
I thought for a split second I'd seen your *Doppelgänger.*

As it were. For when he glanced up and met my eye, his face
was unreadable. It was as if he had just come to

as you had gone away. What is it in us that makes us
see another in another? All the way to Dresden

I could see you when I shut my eyes, remembering you
as you were — this wordless annunciation of yourself

clothed momentarily in the body of another,
thinking in another language had you been spoken to —

as strange to me as when I first saw you in your own flesh,
as we go with each other as we have done, fro and to.

Rue Daguerre

I turned to where your mouth should have been but you were
    not there.
The dream I'd found you in faded like breath from a mirror.

I must be in your former apartment in Montparnasse,
I thought, abed on the uppermost floor under the eaves.

Chestnut candles were flickering at the dormer window.
Light dappled the parterres and borders of the patchwork quilt,

and I remembered how you once thought the quilt was Paris,
the *quartiers* demarcated by pattern and colour.

You had it all mapped out. October was a crisp apple
bitten, with that nip in the air you walked straight out into.

We would meet in the yellowed light of a daguerreotype
of Paris, by the silent fountain in the empty square,

our rendezvous untroubled by any living presence,
since the camera fails to capture anything that moves.

The Story of Madame Chevalier

The swallow flew to my ear from her nest under the eaves.
She told me a stranger was approaching through the forest.

So I climbed to the top of my tall tower and looked out
to see if it was you returning after seven years.

I found you in a clearing. You had changed. But not so much
I didn't know you under the ruin of your cocked hat.

It was evident your memory had been shot to pieces
in the war. You didn't know me from Eve. I took you home.

I bandaged you and bedded you until you got better.
It took you a good nine months not to look at me awry.

Only then did you see the quilt I'd wrapped you in aright.
There are bits of me in here, you said. This must be your work.

I tore up your old shirts the day you enlisted, I said,
and sewed the scraps back together in this crazy pattern.

Before

You stepped out from the shadows wearing a linen jacket
I'd never seen you in before, buttoned on the wrong side.

A sere-cloth dipped in oak-gall ink with buttons of black jet.
A clasp of ebony on the open book in your hands.

Characters of archaic Hebrew Gothic dazzled the page,
black stars danced in the blank universes between the lines,

your mouth disgorging a stream of language not known to me
or any man, for all I knew of what had gone before.

You fingered the stitching of the bespoke jacket and asked
would I like to try it on. But how would it ever fit?

We were not the same dimensions, and of opposite sex.
In this realm every size fits every body, you said.

You put the book away and spoke in a language I knew
from a long time before. We are entering a forest,

you said, whose trees have ears and mouths that listen and
    respond
to every passerby. Everything gets reported back.

And in the forest there is a meadow by a river
that can only be found by someone who has lost their way.

By happenstance we'll go into a little palace there,
the table laid by invisible hands, the rooms prepared.

When what's on the menu is eaten you'll know who you are.
You understand? I nodded not knowing whether I did.

I came to life in a room where a nurse watched over me.
I took her for you when she took off her sere-cloth jacket.

I put it on. It's as if it was made for me, I said.
If so, you said, the pattern was cut before you were born.

It belonged to my grandfather who was shot in the war,
and buried in a cemetery which no longer exists.

The Present

Nice watch, I said. Isn't it? you said, Omega, pre-War.
And still running like a dream after what, fifty-odd years?

Twenty-three jewels. If you open up the back and look
at the movement, you'll see how perfectly it fits its case.

Lovely work: levers, bearings, ratchets, gears, wheels, screws
   and springs
performing their task of intricate synchronicity.

Lovely case: gold bezel, black guilloche enamel inlay.
Original crown. Original black silk ribbon band.

Butterfly clasp. You turned your wrist to show me as you spoke.
You know your watches, I said. Everything I know, you said,

I got with the watch. It was a present from my uncle.
He collected watches. He'd make up stories about them

when I came to visit. At least I think he made them up.
One I remember in particular, a pocket watch

with a dent in its case he said had saved a soldier's life.
The hands had seized at the hour and minute the bullet struck.

Then there was the watch that once belonged to an ace pilot,
found still ticking away in the wreckage of his aircraft,

the Seamaster chronograph of a master mariner,
the Longines of a former winner of the Tour de France.

And I'd picture these men with their handsome, smiling faces,
every one of them dead even then. You fell silent then.

And your watch, does it have a story? I said. Yes, you said,
it belonged to my aunt who had died for the Résistance.

But other people whispered of her collaboration.
If watches could speak, he would say, what tales could they not t

You looked at your watch. Look after this watch for life, he said,
and the watch will still be working long after you are gone.

The Anniversary

What a beautiful watch! she said. Yes, he said, Omega,
this year's model. White gold bezel, black guilloche enamel.

At least that's what it said in the Omega catalogue.
Guilloche, that's the inlay, she said, see? It's a vine pattern.

She held it to her ear. It's guaranteed for life, he said.
She draped the black silk ribbon of the strap over her wrist.

She buckled the butterfly clasp and adjusted the case
to the hollow in her wrist, admiring the way it looked.

Then she held it for him to see. Yes, he said, it's lovely.
It sits very well on you. I think you made a good buy,

she said. Well, he said, this make was recommended to me
by a guy who knows watches. It's the last word in watches.

Omega. The gift of a lifetime. Look after it well,
it'll still be working when both of us are gone, he said.

Filling the Blank

I could use that in my piece, I said to him *à propos*
of the Mont Blanc. Take, for instance, the white star on the peak.

Did you know there was a church in Dresden called Our Lady
of the Snows? And isn't it funny it's snowing tonight?

I envisage some paragraphs on Dresden under snow,
the reconstructed domes and steeples beginning to blur

in the twilight. Then perhaps a *Bierkeller* interior.
I'm drinking a hot schnapps in the heat of a gas-fired stove.

I'm the lady who's deep in small talk with a professor
of music in Dresden the spiritual home of Bach.

She dines that night with the string quartet after the event.
She walks the moonlit esplanade of the Elbe before

retiring to her hotel room where she writes all she has
done that day in her journal with a ladies' Mont Blanc pen.

Peace

Back then you wouldn't know from one day to the next what
    might
happen next. Everything was, as it were, provisional,

slipping from the unforeseeable into tomorrow
even as the jittery present became history.

What kinds of times are these, you'd say, when a conversation
is deemed a crime because it includes so much that is said?

And all the unanswered questions of those dark days come back
to haunt us, the disabled guns that still managed to kill,

the witnesses that became ghosts in the blink of an eye.
Whom can we prosecute when no one is left fit to speak?

I read in this morning's paper, you said, of a stables
in England which had been set on fire. An eyewitness spoke

of horses whinnying, of hooves battering on the doors,
doors padlocked and bolted against all possible escape.

In the Dark

Tell me again about your sojourn in Dresden, I said.
On my way to meet the professor I had a feeling

someone was following me, you said, but when I looked round
no one was there. I was to get the microfilm that night.

I kept singing into myself to keep my courage up.
You know that song, *La nuit s'approche et mon village . . . ?*

. . . s'endort là-bas silencieux, I said. Yes, you said.
And I kept wondering what the canister might contain,

whatever it might be that I was not supposed to know.
I was merely the vehicle, as was the professor.

Though for all I know he might have been a double agent.
Anyway, I sat at the table for hours. No one came.

Just before I reached the hotel I looked back, and I swear
there were footprints in the snow that had not been there before.

Je Reviens

Nice perfume, I said. Yes, you said, the last time I saw you.
What is it about it? I said. The House of Worth, you said,

1932. My mother would have been seventeen.
It's the scent GIs in Paris would buy for their girlfriends

as a promise that they would return when demobilized.
That some did not goes without saying. *I come again,*

Je reviens. The overall effect is difficult
to describe, since it seems to develop separately

but simultaneously on two distinct levels, wavelengths
of suggestion and risk as well as definite statement.

One factor is mysterious and woody, with piquant
flashes of herbs, the other a heady rush of flowers.

It is based on *narcissus poeticus,* a native
of the underworld attractive to ghostly reflections.

Iris root is an essential ingredient, Iris
a sister of the Harpies, and messenger of the gods,

who ferries the souls of dead women to the underworld,
who personifies the rainbow, the iris of the eye.

How we got from the scent to the Afghan rug I don't know,
but as we sprawled carelessly on its ground of red madder

we began to enter its arabesques of indigo
and purpurin flecked with yellow larkspur of the desert.

At first the pattern seemed to be a Tree of Life, but then
the warp and weft began to shift and shimmer under us,

becoming now a dragon and phoenix in combat, now
a snarl of vines or snakes. Ensnarled and thinking to escape,

we plunged down through the ages till we landed on a field
of Afghan war rug bright with helicopters, guns and tanks.

Zugzwang

As the negotiators end by drawing up a form
of words which can be claimed by both sides as a victory;

as on a factory floor in the former East Berlin
the puzzle women puzzle together the shredded files;

as the door handle is sprinkled with fingerprint powder
to trace the guilty hand among so many innocent;

as the old chess master cannot say if ever he learned
the game, since each new game blossoms with new constellations;

as the choreographer charts out moves on a dance floor
like the chalk marks on a snooker table, play having ceased;

as the mad litigant rummages through his suitcase full
of ancient carbon copies to pursue his dubious suit —

so I write these words to find out what will become of you,
whether you and I will be together in the future.

PART TWO

Second Time Round

La nuit s'approche et mon village s'endort là-bas
silencieux . . . You were singing me that song again,

and I was trying to remember where I'd heard it last.
I could see the little church under the Alps at nightfall,

and snow falling beyond the casement window where you sat
with a vase of blue flowers on the table beside you.

Night was approaching the parlour as it did the village
in the words of the song. The world beyond the glass was blurred.

But you had gone elsewhere, back to when I first heard it sung.
It would have been in Paris all of thirty years ago.

It was dusk. *L'heure bleue,* you said, the hour of assignations.
Do you remember how the dim gongs of an Angelus

came booming in from the fog, just as I came to the end?
Echoing the bell in the song? you said. The stroke of six.

It must be that time of the year when it gets dark early,
and I am learning to drive on the wrong side of the road

in your Renault 5 Alpine. I shift the unfamiliar
gears. You should pretend to be me, you say, picture yourself

in my shoes, whereon I begin to imagine the rest,
the *broderie anglaise* bodice and the blue pencil skirt

and the black stockings. I'm wearing one of your vintage hats.
I'm beginning to like this role, I say, as I change up

and find myself on a boulevard which is deserted,
silent save for the swish of our tyres and windscreen wipers.

If I'm you, who are you? I say, whereupon you reply
with a smile I have to take my eyes off the road to catch

when a man looms into the windscreen in a split second,
rain pouring from his glistening black ulster and black helmet.

Hotel del Mar

You're lying on top of the quilt in a pane of moonlight.
You've opened the window for the pale voile curtains to stir

in the breeze off the white horses foundering on the shore.
You're thinking of me in a city an ocean away,

reverberations bringing to mind the helicopter
which might hover at my roof as it does on a column

of noise. You can see me lying in our shuttered bedroom.
You think I must be thinking of you, and then of the sound

of the waves. I could be you staring at the blue ceiling
dappled by wavering waves in which — like Leonardo

hearing every possible babble in a peal of bells —
I hear the syllables of your name repeated, Nina,

until the helicopter withdraws its barrage of noise,
the waves receding to a murmur as we fall asleep.

On the Contrary

It's because we were brought up to lead double lives, I said.
Yes, you said, because of the language thing it was one thing

with my father, another with my mother. Father tongue
and mother tongue, all the more so when they separated

irrevocably. It seems they could not live together.
I stayed with my mother and would visit him at weekends.

Yet something else was going on, and I remember times
when the phone would remain unanswered when it rang and
    rang.

I dared not pick it up. I see it gleaming and trembling
on its table in the vestibule beside the ashtray

in which one of my mother's cigarette ends lay crushed, tipped
with her red lipstick and still smoking. I go to her room

where I know she will hold me and speak some words of English
before lapsing into her mother tongue and mine. She smells

of cigarette smoke, tears and perfume. This is the heirloom,
the quilt we're lying on now that I lay on then with her.

She sings of the little village in the Alps where snow falls
eternally, and friends leave friends in the gathering dusk.

She was never outspoken. You can see how the patchwork
might resemble that country in summer, with its bright fields

and the crooked white seams of its intervening roadways.
I would travel them dreamily before I fell asleep.

And what of your father? I said. Oh, he lived by himself,
though I suspect there was another woman on the go,

you said. Sometimes I thought I could smell a foreign perfume.
I'd think the room would be empty but for him when I'd gone.

And I'd see him at the other end of the phone, staring
at his watch, wondering if it is the right time to ring.

Treaty

I grew up between languages, not knowing which came first.
My mother spoke one tongue to me, my father another.

They used both with each other, sometimes both at the same tir
and sometimes I would think this was a language of their own.

With visitors we spoke the language of the visitors,
be they doctors, neighbours, relations, clergy or police.

When I learned to write, that was another language again.
I said the words under my breath as I traced the letters.

So you spoke as if from a long way off and long ago.
Why are you telling me all this? I said. Only because

I remember the first time I spoke to you on the phone.
You told me how glad you were to hear the sound of my voice.

Whether I spoke to you in my first language when I said
I loved you, I don't know, but I do know the words were true.

Redoubt

I stared at my face for an age in the en suite mirror.
Then I must have crawled into bed before my mind went blank.

The next morning when I went down for breakfast he was there.
He asked if he could join me and I could hardly say no.

He looked different in daylight, his face was more open,
though he still wore the two Mont Blanc pens in his breast pocket.

He told me over the black coffee, bread rolls, ham and cheese,
that he had found our dialogue last night most interesting.

But was I really from Ireland? That was hard to believe,
my French was so good. Your French is very good too, you said,

I'd never have guessed you were from where you said you were
    from.
What would you have taken me for had you not known? he said.

Oh, definitely a business man, but what kind of business?
I would have thought from the pens that you were into writing.

But writing what? Manuals, statutes, orders, agendas?
You didn't strike me as a writer of fiction, you said.

You said you thought he looked at you twice but he said nothing.
But for the two of us the white dining room was empty.

Knives glittered on the linen. The silence was palpable
before the waiter entered and asked if we had finished.

He began to clear away the remains of our breakfast.
The agent looked at me and I looked back at him, you said.

Yes, you said, and you sat staring at each other across
an empty table. Sunlight glittered on the stained linen.

Your eyes dropped. Still he said nothing. When I looked up,
   he'd gone.
I went to pack and check out. I never saw him again.

I looked at you. I wonder what became of him, you said,
looking into my eyes as you once might have done with him.

The Assignation

Something like that happened to me once abroad, I said. I
had walked the mile to the railway station from the harbour,

my steps seemingly followed by the tolling of a bell
and what sounded like far-off, sporadic bursts of gunfire

through darkening streets where half the shopfronts were
    boarded up.
By the time I entered the buffet I was ravenous.

The menu was written in a language I couldn't read.
I found the serving-girl staring at me questioningly —

she could have been your sister, so familiar were her eyes —
so I pointed to what looked like a baguette with *jambon*,

almost disappointed when it turned out to be just that.
She watched me wash it down with a glass of the local beer.

Vous êtes étranger? she said, sounding Eastern European.
Nodding I told her in school French where I was from and where

I might have been. I did not know the right times for the train.
You can depend on them, she said, to run after midnight.

I heard the shriek of a train tearing the darkness apart,
the landscape it moved through a world away from the city,

and I thought you might indeed fulfil the assignation
though I could not remember whose decision it had been

to meet as designated strangers on a bare platform.
Perhaps it was determined in some other waking life.

I became aware of the station clock in the mirror,
and watched the second hand tick inexorably backwards.

When I came to I saw your face in the serving-girl's face
and I looked into her eyes, unquestionably your eyes,

and saw fleeting in their depths a world where we never met,
both of us blind to each other and what we would become.

Revolution

The spinning mills going up in an avalanche of flame.
The vacillating gun-turret of the Saracen tank.

The tick and tack of the Remote Bomb Disposal Unit.
The watch you consult to see what has elapsed of the day.

The untrustworthy public clocks, stopped at various times.
The hands sometimes missing or the face pockmarked by
    shrapnel,

the face-powder compact they discovered in your handbag.
The hands at my spreadeagled body, ankles, hips and groin.

The clicking security cameras watching, watching.
The helicopter trawling the murk with its wand of light.

The public telephone box where I'm trying to get through.
The helicopter hovering on its down-swash of noise.

The way your voice comes over in waves of long-distance call.
The things you tell me of what might become of us for now.

Through

Irrevocable: five syllables like rapid handclaps
or a volley of gunshots. Then I told you he was dead.

How did it happen? I couldn't say what reason they had,
or if indeed it was random, else someone else was meant.

I could see him standing next to me in the school yearbook.
I picture the faces of all those others now absent,

some by cancer, some by heart attack, some by suicide,
some by combatants unknown or known, if not by default —

all of us blind to what would become of what we had been.
What turn did I take that led me to meet you when I did?

Open the yearbook. Pretend you're the camera taking
me in for that shuttered second when I look straight through you

As if you were alive in my eyes then as I am now,
as if I remembered what you looked like before or since.

Pas de Deux

I opened the oak doors of the armoire and stepped inside.
Your clothes still hung there, perfumed with memories of perfumes.

The nub of the lavender tweed, the nap of the linen.
The black sheen of a pansy-blue velvet rubbed the wrong way.

The blue pencil skirt you bought in Second Time Round under
the matching blue jacket you bought in Double Exposure.

The boxes of hats from Déjà Vu and Pandora's Chest.
The boxes of gloves from La Belle Époque and New to You.

The blouses of pale blue cotton next to the sheer linens
purchased in Second Début, Turnstyle, or Another Time.

And I remember you in Generations or Good Byes
trying on whatever piece behind a half-draped curtain,

my standing at the pier mirror looking at you askance,
as you watched me admiring the cut of your present clothes.

Second Hand

I have your watch before me, your aunt's pre-War Omega,
thirty, forty years older than me and still running strong.

I'm winding it up as I have every day for a year.
I listen to it closely to hear time ticking away.

I see how it nestles in the hollow between your bones,
how your wrist bears the ghost of a strap when you take it off.

It's the first thing you take off. Then you dim the Dresden lamp.
I kiss the pale weal left by the buckle on a blue vein.

I remember how you wore your watch when driving, facing
inward for your glance as you manoeuvred the Citroën,

a midnight blue vintage Déesse you'd picked up for a song.
You drove too fast. I'd wonder how long it would be before

they'd pull you from the wreck of the immobilized Déesse,
and know by its sweeping hand that your watch was still working

Le Mot Juste

Still the interminable wrestle with words and meanings.
Flaubert labouring for days over a single sentence.

The deaf Beethoven scribbling over what he's just written
with a blunt quill plucked from the innards of a harpsichord.

The skeins of stuff from which your family history is spun,
and what wheels there are within wheels within your vintage watch.

Your widow aunts discussing the quilt at their quilting bee
following the dips and gradients of its staggered repeats.

The way the bread is full of unrepeatable bubbles
when you pull it apart and fathom its interior.

Snow falling interminably, irrevocably on
the little village in a song your mother used to sing.

Still the interminable struggle with words and meanings.
These words foundering for now over a single sentence.

Proposal

It happened over an apple. We were in a market,
sunshine and August showers flickering through the glazed roof

over a barrel of apples, green with a blush of red,
the dew still seeming to glisten on them. You picked one up.

Try it and see, Miss, said the vendor. You nodded, and bit
into the crisp flesh. You felt its juice explode in your mouth

as I did when you passed it to me for the second bite.
They're called Discovery, said the vendor, a very good

eating apple. We bought a pound of them, some wine and cheese
and repaired to the country where we picnicked by a stream.

You offered me a Discovery. This time I could taste
your mouth from it through the juice. We took bite for bite
    from it

until we finished it as one. We threw away the core.
Then we asked things of each other we'd never asked before.

The Shadow

The Glass Bead Game? I said. *Das Glasperlenspiel,* if you like,
you said, not that my German is anything to speak of.

Though I remember, as a verb, *perlen* means to bubble,
as in upwardly streaming pearls of water in a pot

just coming to the boil. As for what went on in the book,
I'm at a loss to say what it was all about, or not.

The game itself was difficult to visualize. I thought
of a chess more infinitely complicated than chess,

played in three dimensions, if not four or five, for the game,
as I understood it, could admit of most anything,

though politics was frowned on. The game was above all that.
A Bach motet, or how the prose style of Julius Caesar

mirrors the cadences of some Early Byzantine hymns,
the calligraphic gestures of a flock of birds at dusk:

these were considered subjects for the Glass Bead Game. Or not.
There were always those who thought the opposite to be true.

The subject of the book becomes a *Magister Ludi,*
Master of the Game. He is skilled in many disciplines.

With a luminous gold stylus he writes a hieroglyph
on the dark, and so initiates a constellation

from which blossom countless others. Were the Game a music,
it would require an organ with an infinite number

of manuals, pedals and stops. If geometry, or not,
Pythagoras never dreamed of it. Plato was not close.

Though it originated in the simple abacus,
the wires representing a musical staff and the beads

of various sizes, shapes and colours of glass the notes,
it grew in time to be a model of the universe.

I gather the glass beads became metaphorical beads,
not to be fingered by hand but tuned to some other sense.

At any rate, a Master is not allowed to marry.
Now I remember this one was called Knecht, which means not
    knight,

but vassal. He is in thrall to the Game. He is assigned
an underling, a Shadow. The Shadow must study him.

It does not do for a Master to have a weak Shadow.
And the Master must be fit to stand up to his Shadow.

Though the Shadow may act in his master's stead, he may not
lay forward proposals of his own. And though he may wear

the Master's robes when occasion demands he can never
be Master himself. Such are the rules of the Glass Bead Game.

So you must cultivate your Shadow, for there is never
one Master, but another lies waiting in his shadow,

you said. And what has all of this got to do with Berlin,
I said, and your time there? You don't know how much I missed

I kept wondering where you were and what you were thinking.
As did I of you, you don't know the half of it, you said.

Isn't that the trouble? That I don't know the half of it?
Sometimes I wonder if we speak the same language, I said.

You took a sip of cold coffee and stared out the window.
The sun had just come out. Leaf-shadow dappled the cobbles.

It's like this, you said. Those who play the Glass Bead Game don't know
there's a war on they're so wrapped up in themselves and their Game.

You know I was in Berlin for a reason. Yes, I chose
to walk that path, as surely as I chose to go with you.

There's no point in going into what else I might have been.
Then you walked out the door and I followed in your shadow.

The Fetch

I woke. You were lying beside me in the double bed,
prone, your long dark hair fanned out over the downy pillow.

I'd been dreaming we stood on a beach an ocean away
watching the waves purl into their troughs and tumble over.

Knit one, purl two, you said. Something in your voice made me
   think
of women knitting by the guillotine. Your eyes met mine.

The fetch of a wave is the distance it travels, you said,
from where it is born at sea to where it founders to shore.

I must go back to where it all began. You waded in
thigh-deep, waist-deep, breast-deep, head-deep, until you
   disappeared.

I lay there and thought how glad I was to find you again.
You stirred in the bed and moaned something. I heard a footfall

on the landing, the rasp of a man's cough. He put his head
around the door. He had my face. I woke. You were not there.

Second Take

I remember the first time you telephoned me, you said.
Telephoned, I said, isn't that terribly old-fashioned?

And I pictured myself in a red kiosk, the black phone
crooked to my neck, as, earpiece to ear and mouthpiece to mouth,

I drop money into the slot of the clunking coin-box.
I press button B when I hear you speaking and I say,

Is that you? Yes, you say, it's me, didn't you know my voice?
You know what the voice is? you said. What is the voice? I said.

A closed-tube resonator, like the canal of the ear,
you said. The vocal column begins in the vocal folds,

which pucker like lips on the mouthpiece of a saxophone.
Every voice can be voiceprinted like a musical score

and can be used to prove you did a crime of which you spoke.
That's why I knew your voice then. And you're speaking in it now.

Corrigendum

Did I say button B? It should have been A. Button B
was the one you pressed to get your money back when no one

lifted the receiver from its cradle. You imagine
a room empty with the instrument's repeated trilling,

sunlight vacillating over an unmade patchwork quilt,
or someone listening under its eaves to the distant noise.

I hate to leave a phone unanswered, but I must attend
to its summons there and then, even if it means climbing

the long stair to the lumber room where the tall pier mirror
reflects a rocking horse and two armies of toy soldiers

facing each other across an Afghan rug which trembles
as I walk on it to the red box and lift the black phone.

Why are you not in the room when you told me you would be?
I call three times. There is no answer. I press Button B.

Fall

I'm Miranda, you said, though some people call me Nina.
Gabriel, I said, though some people call me Gabriel.

Why Nina? Why not? you said. A rose by any other
et cetera. You bore the scent of a nameless perfume.

We were sequestered in The Crown after the explosion,
illuminated by the emerald and ruby glass

of its famed windows. You'd never seen anything like it,
carved heraldic beasts gazing at you from the reredos.

You were telling me how you wrote about other places,
places usually more peaceful than this, but with a past.

You remembered a church gable pockmarked with bullet holes,
the celebration of bells that set off an avalanche,

words that put us in mind of the ever-toppling windows,
pigeons rising in a blue and emerald thundercloud

to fill the sky above the newly blasted premises
and turn a city caught unawares into onlookers.

You wanted to know whom I thought might be responsible
in such a way as to intimate you'd been here before.

I was born here, you said. My father travelled in linen.
But when I was seven we removed to his part of France.

He'd tell me stories of the War and the Liberation,
of how he met my mother in a crowd of laughing girls,

girls in high wedge-heeled platform shoes and Pompadour
    hairstyles,
blowing kisses everywhere, garlanding the tank turrets.

By now the gaslight had flickered on in dim pearly globes
and I was about to tell you about my mother's War

when there was a general hush for the News coming on,
all eyes swivelling to watch it again in slow motion.

L'Air du Temps

That whiff of L'Air du Temps I got back then in the wardrobe —
I remember when I first registered that primal scent,

whence the symbolism of the pair of intertwining doves,
and the frosted glass bottle that made you think of Paris

under a cloudless winter sky, as I did of your blouse
of pale pastel blue, so crisp and clean and near transparent.

Then it began to develop waves, and I was standing
with you on a beach as we noted how the laps of foam

mouthed upon one another, how the crest of the barrel
doubled and broke into a shrubbery of jumping sprays.

We got soaked with spindrift and spray, our cheeks frosted with
    brine,
but we saw the waves well. In the sunlight they were green-blue,

flinty sharp, and rucked in straight lines by the wind, bottle-green
under their forelocks, or the turned-over plait of the crest.

The laps of running comb buffeting the sea wall doubled
on themselves, plied and purled in their folded crash and back-swash,

clocking the stones underwater against one another.
We leaned unsteadily into the wind all the way back

to the hotel. We stood and looked at the waves for a while
from the bay window. We switched off the lights to watch TV.

They were showing the latest news from my native city.
It looked like a Sixties newsreel where it always drizzled,

the police wearing glistening black ulsters and gun-holsters.
When it came to the bit with the talking heads we switched off.

We must have drifted off to the far-off sound of the waves,
both of us thinking of how, when taking off your jersey

of rib-knitted wool in the dark, with an accidental
stroke of your finger you drew a flash of electric light.

Never Never

Once upon a time there was a little boy, let's call him
Gabriel, you said. The tale begins in a girl's bedroom.

Gabriel flies in the window. He's looking for something.
He rummages in a chest of drawers and finds the shadow

that was snipped from his feet when the window slammed shut
on him
the last time he ventured there. He's trying to stick it back on

with soap when the girl wakes. Poor boy, you need a woman's
touch,
she says, and she sews back the shadow with needle and thread.

You may kiss me now, she says. What's a kiss? says the boy. So
she gives him a thimble instead. He gives her an acorn.

He teaches her to fly. Have I heard this story before?
I said. Oh, probably, you said. Let's forget the story.

We drank the last of the good wine and tumbled into bed.
Then you gave me a thimble and I gave you an acorn.

Birthright

You ask what's in a name? Where I come from it tells you where
you're from, I said, whether this allegiance or the other.

But you can always change your name, you said. Not where I'm
   from,
I said, that would be considered a collaboration.

Or rather, an apostasy. The act of a turncoat.
In any case, they'll find you out no matter what, for there

are other indicators of identity. Such as?
you said. Colour and cut of clothes, I said, the way you talk

and what you talk about, the way you walk, your stance, or how
you look askance, the set and colour of your eyes and hair.

Just look at you, you said, you're talking through your hat. Look at
what you're wearing, that good Protestant Harris tweed jacket.

The black serge waistcoat a linen broker might have cast off.
The grandfather shirt no grandfather of yours ever wore.

Collaboration

Eventually you sank back into the deep well of sleep.
You'd been telling me about one of your aunts or great-aunts,

or rather the family whispers you'd heard over the years.
She managed to dress stylishly even during the War.

She wore nylons and seemed to have a secret cache of scent.
Where her airs and graces came from no one ventured to know.

What brought it all to mind was a dream you had woken from.
You were in Paris, disembodied and invisible,

swooping round the Eiffel Tower and down the Invalides.
You glimpsed her walking by the Seine. You glided behind her.

You knew by the cut of her clothes it was 1940.
Before you knew it you entered her clothes and became her.

And you found yourself walking, walking, as the church bells
    tolled
and tolled, announcing the hour of your next assignation.

From Your Notebook

I am waiting for you to call tonight and you do not.
I sit and watch the dumb telephone and will it to ring.

I walked all day through the replicated streets of Dresden
thinking of you just as I walked in the footsteps of Bach.

I'm using the dressing table as a dummy keyboard
as I write. One of his more simple fugues, if you must know.

I follow the curve of one of its recurrent figures
trying to figure out the resolution that is never

there in any proper fugue of Bach's. Melodic fragments,
perpetually unfinished, that seems to have been his style.

If you must know, I'm not writing this with a Mont Blanc pen.
I refused it when the agent took it from his pocket.

He must have thought I was willing enough to begin with.
The telephone rings and I let it ring and ring and ring.

Prelude and Fugue

Regarding the zoo where a keeper was running amok
among the burning monkeys and the teetering giraffes,

I'd read Vonnegut's *Slaughterhouse 5*, so it rang a bell,
I said. And I'd gleaned from my mother's memories of the Blitz

how the German aeroplanes would drop magnesium flares,
the whole sky lit up by dozens of ghostly, silver lights

floating down on silk parachutes. They were like Christmas trees,
she said. The two opposing persuasions would take refuge

in the fields that lay beyond the city, lying hugger-
mugger under the blossoming hawthorn trees in couples

of each other, until the all-clear, blossoming of smoke
above the city. Then a church bell began to toll, then

another and another, as if keeping to a score
of harmony and dissonance, for thee, for thee, for thee.

The Story of the Chevalier

You wore a red halter dress and a white comb I thought bone.
A diminutive whistle hung on a chain from your neck.

You took me by candlelight to a room under the eaves.
I said I thought I'd seen the patchwork quilt somewhere before.

It's a very old pattern, you said, Cathedral Windows.
My four aunts made it, having been made widows by the War.

They pieced back together the light of the shattered windows.
They saw themselves walking again down a shimmering aisle.

Before I knew it you were holding me under the quilt.
I found you, my arms around you, even more becoming.

When it was over you turned on a lamp at the window.
You took the little whistle from its chain around your neck.

You asked if I would like to blow on it. I would, and did.
And with that I heard the horse whinnying under the eaves.

To

So engrossed was I by the story of your encounter
I found myself to be looking at the world through your eyes

and pictured the man who looked like me emerge, as he might,
from a mirror at the end of a hotel corridor.

So you will understand I was only an onlooker
in all of this, and not there in my actual body,

the way it happens perchance in dreams. Some nights I'd go back
to see my parents before they had contemplated me.

They would look through me to the flowered bedroom wallpaper
I remember studying before I could speak, seeing

in its arboured trellises a route to the other world
where things that bore no name looked to each other, as they
    would,

for any hint of a family resemblance, reaching out
to touch each other in lieu of words. Your man my double

was like that. I watched him jiggle the key in the wrong lock
before he made his way to another and opened it.

I glided behind. All was dark beyond the vestibule.
He fumbled for and turned on the light switch from memory.

When he went to sit on the bed with his head in his hands
I sat beside him, making no impression on the quilt.

I watched while he poured a drink at the vanity unit.
He looked at himself in the mirror and began to talk

as if to himself, but really it was I, putting words
into his mouth, for I had been there before long ago.

I knew what it was like to inhabit that strange country.
I knew he longed to speak to you, if only long-distance.

But instead he would dream of his young father and mother
looking briefly through him before turning over to sleep.

Rue Daguerre

Later I'd picture you in the rue Daguerre apartment,
standing at the balcony window gazing at Paris

spread out before you like the parterres of the patchwork quilt.
I'd walk over to you and put my hands around your waist.

I'd look over your shoulder to see what you are seeing
through the blaze of the chestnut trees to the crowded avenues.

Crowds used to mean trouble, you'd say, your back still turned
   to me,
back in the Sixties. *La Révolution.* Then we'd kiss

as we sank to our knees to the floor on a Persian rug,
there to enter its intricate, intimate palaces.

At one of the exits we'd find your dark blue Déesse
awaiting with her engine ticking over like a watch.

We'd drive off into the night to arrive at rue Daguerre
in time to see the couple who make love at the window.

The Story of Madame Chevalier

You remember the Incredible Shrinking Man? I said.
Well, last night I dreamed I was him. It began the same way.

The shirt cuffs were the first thing that came to my attention,
drooping down over my knuckles in the bedroom mirror.

And my waistband and shoes were getting looser by the day.
Within weeks you could perch me on your knee like a male doll.

Later you would put me to bed in the empty matchbox.
You failed to watch for the spider that came to explore me.

I fought her with a darning needle, a button my shield.
She retreated from me on a thread. I followed her down

to the cellar. How I made my way back I'll never know.
It took me days to travel over the quilt to your hand.

No longer a hand but an Alpine range of sleeping flesh.
I crawled into an open pore and entered your bloodstream.

Before

Before the War, before my father met my mother, what
went on? you'd say, looking at me as if I had a clue.

Take the jacket I'm wearing, you said, it's 1920s,
it must bear the atmosphere it breathed then, all those perfumes

that beguiled the innocent and the not-so-innocent.
The milliners were in full swing with feathers and velour,

perfumes wafting from perfumeries, and all of Paris
radiant beneath the April blue, flower stalls galore.

No more the horrors of Verdun, the Somme and Passchendaele.
Black Americans are playing jazz in the cabarets.

And the blue hours are full of assignations, though I think
the woman who wore this was a little *sérieuse*.

A very sensible cut, really, for the times, though now
it might be considered *outré*. As for the hat? You shrugged.

That's the problem, you said, most people think you eccentric.
But fashions fade, style is eternal. They made things well then,

even the cheaper garments are of better quality
than you'd get now. I know what you mean, I said. Take the hat,

I said. It's still all right for women to wear hats, but men?
Most men wouldn't be seen dead in a hat. Do you know why?

It's all because of Kennedy. The President, I mean.
Before him you could walk down Wall Street on a sea of hats.

When Kennedy burst on to the scene, bareheaded, handsome,
dressed impeccably in a slim two-buttoned suit, smiling

that broad smile, asking what they could do for America,
sober men threw off their hats in their hundreds and thousands.

But then Kennedy was shot, you said, remember? And men
still won't be seen dead in hats, unless they join an army.

The Present

You were still wearing the watch I'd bought you for your birthday —
a 1949 Rolex Oyster Perpetual

in rose gold and stainless steel with luminous numerals
I knew you'd wanted. You wanted a man's watch for a change,

for all that you loved your ladies' Omegas and Longines.
I think men and women run to different times, you'd say.

I'm wondering if I wore a man's watch would I speed up,
perhaps we might become synchronized. But you drive too fast,

I'd say, and you often look at your watch as you do so,
as if you could never get fast enough to wherever

you're going. You count the hours in minutes as you would miles.
Remember us driving through France as the cocks were crowing?

By the time we came to Paris the sun was going down.
We parked by your apartment and we climbed the wooden hill.

You opened the door. It seemed we'd been away for a while
as we surveyed the empty rooms. You put a kettle on.

It whistled when its time was up. You looked at your Longines,
such a pretty thing on your wrist in its guilloche bezel.

You looked at me. I think we'll have a cup of coffee first,
you said. You poured and we eyed each other through the tendrils

of coffee aroma that rose from the cups. The seconds
ticked by in the second hand sweep of your second-hand watch.

You must be very tired, I said, after all that driving.
Yes, you said, but not that tired. I have my hidden reserves.

The Oyster is synonymous with its watertight case,
you explained. Perpetual is self-explanatory.

I watched the time go by on your glowing watch as you slept
beside me, not quite as naked as the day you were born.

The Anniversary

Yes, but even an oyster must open from time to time,
I said, don't they feed and breathe? Yes, I suppose so, you said,

but that's not the point. The point is, the world is your Oyster.
And you know to your cost how tightly shut oysters can be.

Then I remembered the oyster knife you stole in Les Halles
from a comprehensively stocked kitchen implement shop.

Then over to rue Montorgueil to ogle the oysters
reclining tight-lipped on their beds of crushed ice and seaweed.

We bought two dozen and some good Sancerre to wash them
    down.
We were celebrating one of our anniversaries.

You opened one with a dab twist. When you gave me the knife
to try my hand slipped and I gashed the knuckle of my thumb.

Before I could protest you put your mouth to the deep cut.
When you raised your head I kissed my blood on your open lips.

Filling the Blank

I'm the lady behind the counter of the Mont Blanc shop
who says what a nice hand when you try out one of her pens.

I'm the lady you write to when she's far away from home
though by the time the letter gets there she might have moved on

I'm the lady in charge of the airport lingerie store
who asks you if there is anything she can help you with.

I'm the lady in question whose dimensions you reveal
to the lady in charge of the airport lingerie store.

I'm the lady you bump into unwittingly before
you know her name or age or what she does for a living.

I'm the lady propped up at the bar beside you, who puts
words into your mouth before you even know what they are.

I'm the lady who sleeps in you until death do you part.
I'm the lady you see in your dreams though she be long dead.

Peace

So carefully did you measure your words it seemed to me
you rarely said what first came to mind. You reserved judgement.

Everything was in the way you said a thing, your manner
and your mannerisms, even the way you cocked your head

spoke volumes. And lately you'd taken to wearing a veil
of an ethereal blue voile with your blue velour hat,

colours we saw later in the glass of the cathedral.
Blue stands for eternity, its gaze plumbs infinity.

To penetrate the blue is to go through the looking glass.
Sometimes its gravity evokes the idea of death.

Insubstantial itself, blue embodies whatever is
caught in it. Sound and shapes disappear in it, you might say.

You'd make a very good negotiator, I would say.
Well, I'm a Gemini, after all, you said. Geminis

see both sides of the question, so they say. We're good at trade.
We're ruled by Mercury, the god of commerce and of thieves.

You know that Mercury was Hermes to the Greeks, the god
of music, messenger to the gods, and the conductor

of dead souls to the underworld. He is the god of sleep
and dreams, and carries a staff of intertwining serpents.

He is the god of roads, of travellers, and of memory.
Whatever you find on the road is a gift of Hermes.

As I remember it, we had just driven to Chartres,
'capital of light and perfume', in your blue Déesse.

And afterwards we drifted away between linen sheets
scented with lavender, rehearsing the momentous day

of our marriage, whenever that might be, empyreal
tomorrow blossoming the more we found each other there.

In the Dark

Irrevocable? Unable to be undone, you said.
Unalterable, in other words, irreversible.

As it turned out, my professor was never seen again.
Perhaps he told me too much, but I was not to know that.

Nothing I could have done would have been any different,
for deeds are irrevocable, if not words. Every time

I remember the words of that song, I think of something
different. *Quand vient le soir après l'orage fuyons . . .*

By now I was in Dresden with you, under the night sky
which seemed to blossom with new constellations as you spoke

to me as you might have done to him then, of this and that.
And he did remind me a little bit of you, you said,

I had taken him at his word when he spoke of music.
Bach died blind, he said, and was buried in an unmarked grave

in St John's, Leipzig. I travelled there by train the next day.
They found his coffin a hundred and fifty years later.

St John's was destroyed by Allied forces in World War Two.
His remains were reburied in St Thomas's, Leipzig.

1949, the year that I was born. He lies there
to this day. Fugue, my professor said, is a kind of trance

in which the victim disappears for years on end, until
he comes to himself in a strange town and quits the double

life he led unbeknownst to himself. In musical terms
the fugue must perform its often stealthy work with shifting

melodic fragments that remain perpetually in
abeyance, or unconsummated, so to speak, you said.

And I think of the blank darkness that descended on Bach
as the music which blazed in his head became forgotten.

Je Reviens

You woke up one morning and said, I must go to Nevers.
You gave me to understand in a manner of speaking

that you'd some longstanding unfinished business in Nevers.
It's like this, you said. You gestured to the Persian carpet

that adorned the floor of your apartment. The Tree of Life
is a family tree. The weavers of carpets are women.

The work is done from memory. Daughter learns from mother,
each remembering the subtle flaws that went before them.

I'm still trying to untangle what happened in Nevers.
Perhaps I fear my mother found the pattern in Nevers.

We took a slow train to make the long journey. My father
was elsewhere on some business or other, as he would be.

For seven nights my mother would tuck me into my side
of the bed. I'd watch her making up from under the sheet.

A spurt of Je Reviens on both wrists, the hat and veil
adjusted just so. Then the gloves, the clutch handbag, the stole.

When to all intents and purposes I was fast asleep
she'd leave. Late one evening the phone rang. I let it ring.

Nothing was said. I'd no idea what was going on.
Last week I got a letter from Nevers that made me think

more than twice of what might have been going on in Nevers.
You must trust me, I have to do this by myself, you said.

Je reviens, you said, I will return within a week —
your last words to me, as I knew by the end of the week.

The phone rang. I picked it up and I knew from the grave voice
they'd found my number in your black notebook. The Déesse

was a write-off. I took the train to Nevers the next day.
I looked at you. They let me pull the sheet over your face.

Zugzwang

As you might hear every possible babble of language
in bells that tumble and peal to celebrate victory;

as the quilters make a pattern of their remnants and rags,
and the jersey, unravelled, becomes a new skein of wool;

as the fugue must reiterate its melodic fragments
in continuously unfinished tapestries of sound;

as the police might have trawled the wreck of your Déesse
in search of the twist in the plot, the point of no return;

as the words of the song when remembered each time around
remind us of other occasions at different times;

as the geographer traces the long fetch of the waves
from where they are born at sea to where they founder to shore —

so I return to the question of those staggered repeats
as my memories of you recede into the future.

Acknowledgements

I am grateful to the editors of the *London Review of Books*, *The New Yorker*, *Poetry London*, *Poetry Review*, *The Times Literary Supplement* and the *Ulster Tatler* in which some of these poems were published first, some under different titles.

I want to thank Sinéad Morrissey for her editorial suggestions, and Paul Nolan whose comments on the work in progress were stimulating and provocative.

I learned the French song from my sister Caitlín some forty years ago. She learned it from a Dominican nun, Sister Mary de Lourdes, in St Dominic's High School, Belfast. I have been unable to trace any other source for it. Shortly after finishing the book I checked the words of the song with Caitlín, whereupon I discovered I had misremembered the last line of the first verse, which should read, *Du jour annonce les adieux* (*Announces the day's farewells*).